Economically Developing Countries

India

David Cumming

Wayland

Contents

India today

India occupies the huge triangle of land poking out of the continent of Asia into the Indian Ocean. It is bordered by six nations: Pakistan, China, Nepal, Bhutan, Bangladesh and Myanmar (previously Burma). Two of its neighbours, Pakistan and Bangladesh, used to be part of India until the country was divided in 1947. India is above the equator, which means it is in the Northern Hemisphere.

India has nearly 17 per cent of all the people in the world. Or, to put it another way, every sixth person in the world is an Indian. Hindi and Bengali, two of India's major languages, are the fifth and sixth most-spoken languages in the world. With India's population fast approaching 900 million, only China has more people.

India is a confusing country. Its scientists and computer experts are among the best, capable of producing the most modern technology and successfully rocketing satellites into space. So it would seem to be a modern, industrialized nation. Yet in no other country do so many people work on the land and live in extreme poverty. For these reasons, India is still considered to be a developing nation.

India has 36 cities, each of which is home to more than 500,000 people. However, the majority of Indian people live in the country where facilities, such as education and health care, are limited.

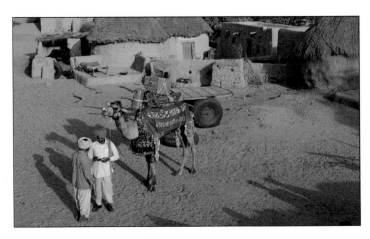

In the desert state of Rajasthan, camels are an important means of transport, used even for delivering the mail.

INDIA AT A GLANCE

Land area	3,287,263 square kilometres
Main cities (population in millions)	Bombay (9.9), New Delhi (7.2), Calcutta (4.4)
Population	884 million (estimate for 1992)
Currency	Rupee, divided into 100 paise
Main languages	Hindi and English, plus 15 regional languages
Longest rivers	Brahmaputra (2,900 km); Ganges (2,510 km)
Highest points	K-2 (8,611 m) and Kangchenjunga (8,598 m)

India has an enormous variety of country including hot, humid jungles in the south, desert in the north-west and the snow-capped Himalayas in the north-east, on the border with China.

Even more perplexing is the fact that India has not always been like this. It used to be prosperous, until it was discovered by Europeans. Then it was colonized by the British, who used its resources to make Britain richer. In 1947, the British gave India its independence, but India by then had become a poor, backward country. Getting India back on its feet has not been easy. Putting right the wrongs of history has been held up by nature and by Indian society itself.

5

The physical environment

India is the seventh-largest country in the world: roughly 3,200 km from top to toe and 2,700 km across at its widest point. People living at the southern tip are as far from New Delhi, the capital, as people in Athens, Greece, are from Londoners in England. Inevitably, communication is difficult within such a big country.

FARMLAND

Poor soils and a lack of water mean that only 55 per cent of India is fit for farming. Deforestation and overgrazing on much of the land have led to the erosion, by wind and rain, of topsoil from the northern highlands and the Deccan plateau. Fertilizers have to be used to encourage plant growth in the thin, stony soil that remains.

The best soil lies on the plains between the Himalayas and the Deccan, across which the River Ganges meanders to the Bay of Bengal. This soil is formed of a deep layer of alluvium, dropped over the centuries by the Ganges and its many tributaries when they flood. The alluvium is good for farming because it is rich in the nutrients that crops such as rice, wheat and vegetables need for good growth.

The most fertile land lies in the river valleys. Here, in the northern state of Ladakh, water from the River Indus is used to irrigate farming land.

THE IMPORTANCE OF THE MONSOON

No matter how good the soil, nothing will grow in it unless it is well watered. The farmers on the Ganges plains are fortunate because plenty of water is available from the river, via irrigation channels, and from under the ground. The rest of India's farmers have to rely on the monsoon for rain.

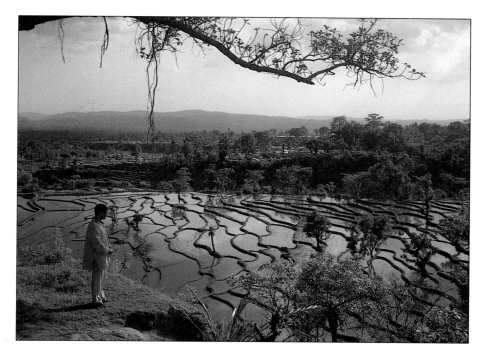

India has three seasons:

• Winter (lasting from October to February) is mostly warm and dry. Although temperatures plunge well below freezing-point in the Himalayas, they average 25 °C in the south.

• Spring (March to May) is hot and dry.

• Summer (June to September) is wet, and very hot, with temperatures soaring to 45 °C.

The monsoon is both a help and a hindrance. Some years it brings so much rain that there are destructive floods in much of India.

The rain is brought by the monsoon, a wind from the south-west. Blowing in from the equator, it picks up moisture over the Indian Ocean. The monsoon soaks the south first, usually around the end of May. Then, at a steady 20 km per hour, it moves across the whole country, reaching the north-west by the middle of July.

CLIMATE

New Delhi			Madras		
Month	Average temp (°C)	Average rainfall (mm)	Month	Average temp (°C)	Average rainfall (mm)
Jan	14	23	Jan	24	36
Feb	17	18	Feb	25	10
March	23	13	March	28	8
April	28	8	April	31	15
May	34	13	May	33	25
June	34	74	June	33	48
July	32	180	July	31	91
Aug	30	173	Aug	31	117
Sept	29	117	Sept	30	119
Oct	26	10	Oct	28	305
Nov	29	3	Nov	26	356
Dec	16	10	Dec	25	140

The monsoon is a mischievous wind, as it does both harm and good. Some years it arrives early and catches everyone unawares with a lot of rain. Floods can drown people and animals, wash away land and property, and generally cause chaos. In September 1980, heavy monsoon rains caused the River Ganges to burst its banks: 1,600 people died, 43,000 villages were flooded, and the city of Calcutta was knee-deep in water. In other years, the monsoon will arrive late and drop hardly any rain. Cattle die of thirst, farmers' fields dry up and people are threatened by food shortages. In between these extremes, there are years when the monsoon brings enough rain for good harvests.

Troublesome though it is, the monsoon is vital to millions of India's farmers. Although it blows for only a few months in the summer, the monsoon brings 70 per cent of all the rain falling on India every year. There is little rain during winter or spring, which means that some areas are dry for eight months of the year. Unless farmers can irrigate their fields during this time, they cannot grow any crops.

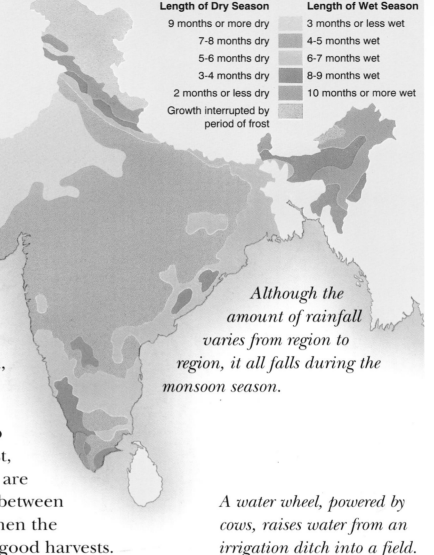

Length of Dry Season	Length of Wet Season
9 months or more dry	3 months or less wet
7-8 months dry	4-5 months wet
5-6 months dry	6-7 months wet
3-4 months dry	8-9 months wet
2 months or less dry	10 months or more wet
Growth interrupted by period of frost	

Although the amount of rainfall varies from region to region, it all falls during the monsoon season.

A water wheel, powered by cows, raises water from an irrigation ditch into a field.

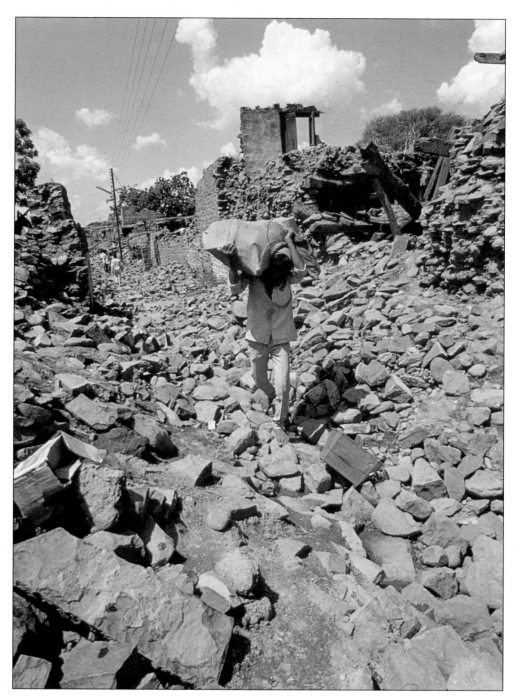

Only 20 per cent of the farm land is irrigated, which means that 80 per cent of Indian farmers rely on the monsoon. They sow their seeds in the spring and harvest their crops, when the rains have stopped. They can grow little food until the following summer, when the monsoon will again provide water for their crops.

Earthquakes are another natural hindrance to India's progress. This man is clearing up after the 1993 earthquake in Maharashtra.

DESTRUCTIVE EARTHQUAKES

Life in India is also disrupted by earthquakes, which are common. On 30 September 1993, an earthquake shook 500 sq km of Maharashtra state. Lasting only seconds, it was powerful enough to kill 7,600 people and 2,100 cattle, to injure a further 217,300 people and completely destroy 18,800 houses. It will cost about £60 million to repair all the damage.

The effects of colonialism

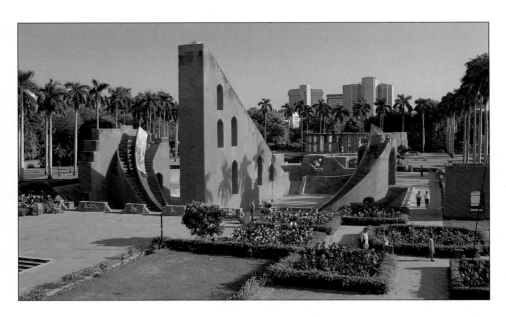

Built in 1725, the Jantar Mantar observatory in New Delhi was used to revise the calendar and to check on ancient astronomical calculations.

Most people think that India benefited from the arrival of Europeans, that they, with their supposedly more advanced ways, generously modernized a backward nation to help the people living there. In fact, the reverse is nearer the truth, since there is much evidence to show that the Europeans did more harm than good to India. Instead of offering India a helping hand, the Europeans, particularly the British, held back India's progress – deliberately.

Europeans came to India in the 1500s to trade and to learn, for in many areas India was ahead of the rest of the world. European astronomers found that their Indian counterparts were using accurate tables for their calculations that had been compiled in 3100BC. They also discovered that Aryabhata, an astronomer working in AD500, knew that the earth was round and that a year lasted 365.3586 days. In 1790, Professor John Playfair of Edinburgh University, Scotland, concluded that astronomical observations were being made in India 'when all Europe was barbarous'.

Indian mathematicians provided the world with the zero, the decimal system, and a method of multiplication used in calculating machines before modern-day computers were invented. They were also working with many algebraic and geometrical formulae well before mathematicians in Europe.

10

In 325BC steel, called *wootz*, started to be made in India, long before it was made anywhere else. The production of *wootz* was complicated, one of the processes requiring temperatures of 1,200 °C. A sample of *wootz* was sent to London in the 1700s, where a scientist at the Royal Society said it was 'decidedly the best [steel] I have yet met with'. In 1842 British metallurgists praised the quality of Indian iron. Later, they were astounded to learn that it was made more efficiently and cheaply than in Britain, where new factories were meant to be the best in the world. A 7 m-tall *wootz* pillar in the Quitab Minar courtyard in Delhi does not have a speck of rust on it, despite having been in the open air since AD500. The reason it is rust-free continues to be a mystery.

Indian society, too, was well organized when the Europeans arrived. The farmers grew sufficient food throughout the year for everyone to be well fed. Their methods were a model of environmental friendliness. Doctors, using centuries-old remedies based on natural, medicinal herbs, kept sickness away. They knew about vaccination long before European doctors.

There was a good education system, with schools within reach of every village. Indeed, when the Europeans arrived, there were probably more literate people in India than in Europe. The arts and three major religions – Hinduism, Islam and Buddhism – flourished. India was far from being a backward country. If anything, the Europeans needed its help, rather than the other way round.

The Quitab Minar's iron pillar is about 1,600 years old. It continues to amaze people because it is free of rust, despite having been in the open air all the time.

THE EAST INDIA COMPANY

On 31 December 1600, the British government gave the East India Company permission to be the only British firm to trade with India. From then on, the company was in charge of selling British goods in India and Indian goods in Britain. It could keep everything it earned from this business. The company's owners were delighted: India was theirs and they could do whatever they liked with it. All they wanted to do with India was to make money from it – lots of money. For the best part of 300 years, the company saw India as a bottomless treasure chest which it could plunder to its heart's content.

The East India Company opened offices and factories in India, which it protected with its own army. Soon the soldiers were being used to conquer Indian rulers who were reluctant to trade with the company. Their lands were then taken over by the company. Eventually, the company was governing much of India. The British considered themselves superior to the Indians and showed them no respect, frequently ill-treating them. The company encouraged its staff to earn as much as possible, irrespective of the suffering they caused.

British Territory by 1805

Protected states

British Territory after 1856

KASHMIR

PUNJAB

RAJPUT LANDS

BENGAL

Calcutta

Bombay

Madras

The British did not directly control all of India, but their influence extended over the entire continent until 1947.

Indian people who defied the British rulers were swiftly put down. This drawing shows some being executed by hanging, and by being fired out of gun barrels.

12

> *'It is a country of inexhaustible riches and one which cannot fail to make its new masters the richest corporation in the world.'*
> **– Robert Clive, top official of the East India Company**

DESTRUCTION OF FARMLAND

The East India Company introduced a high land tax, forcing farmers to pay 50 per cent of their earnings. 'The idea,' as a company manager admitted, 'is to get as much as possible out of the *ryot* [peasant farmer] and when no more is to be got out of him, let him go to the Devil!' Many farmers could not pay the tax, so they sold their property to wealthy landowners, called *zemindars*. The *zemindars* allowed the farmers to remain on their land in return for paying them rent. Farmers who could not afford the rent were thrown off their land. If they were not replaced, the land went to waste. As a result, about 30 per cent of good farming land became useless, and food production fell.

The East India Company also reduced the amount of food grown by forcing farmers to plant cash crops – such as cotton, indigo, tea and jute – which were for selling, not for eating. Previously, enough food had been grown for some to be stored for the years when there was no rain. Now, there was no surplus food to put aside, so there were famines when the monsoon failed. The worst was in 1777, when 10 million people died in Bengal.

One of the worst famines in India's history was in the northern state of Bihar in 1770, where 30 per cent of the people died.

The company cut down many of India's forests to make ships and railway sleepers and so the land could be used for coffee and tea plantations. To ensure there would be enough timber for its needs, the company made laws to keep Indians out of the forests, and introduced a firewood tax. Consequently, cattle dung replaced wood as a cooking fuel. There was less dung to fertilize the soil, so much good farming soil lost its nutrients, and food production declined even further.

The skilled craftsmanship needed to build and to decorate this southern Indian temple shows how advanced India was when the British arrived.

EDUCATION

The East India Company's land reforms also affected the education system. Most schools had been self-financing. They had been given their own land, which they used to grow food for their staff and pupils, as well as a source of income to pay their running costs. The new land tax made this impossible, and many schools had to shut.

All the money raised by taxes went back to Britain. Before these taxes were introduced, this money would have stayed in India. India's raw materials, such as cotton, were also taken back to Britain and not used in India. The East India Company did not develop any industries in India, for fear that they would compete with the factories in Britain. Little was invested in India unless it was absolutely necessary. Much was spent on building railways, but only because they helped the British to get goods to and from the harbours.

In 1784, members of the British parliament, appalled by what had been going on in India, forced the government to shut the East India Company and to take over the running of India itself. By then, it was too late: India had been brought to its knees. Before the British arrived, India had been prosperous and self-sufficient. Now, the majority of its people were landless, ill fed, illiterate and poor. Farming land had been ruined and industries undeveloped.

'We did not conquer India for the benefit of the Indians. We conquered India as the outlet of goods of Great Britain.'
– Lord Brentford, speaking in 1931

14

INDEPENDENCE FROM BRITISH RULE

By the late 1800s, the seeds of dissatisfaction had been sown in India. An independence movement grew and gathered momentum in the 1920s, under the leadership of Mahatma Gandhi. His demands for the British to 'Quit India' and to give Indians *swaraj*, or self-rule, were finally answered in 1947, when India became an independent country.

The British may have left nearly fifty years ago, but India still has not recovered from their unjust, and often cruel, rule. It will take a long time for the scars of colonialism to heal.

By the 1930s, many Indians supported Gandhi in trying to force the British out of India. Here, police break up an anti-British demonstration in Calcutta.

'You have been taught that … British rule in India is beneficial. Nothing is more false! You cannot escape two facts: first, that under the British, India has become the world's poorest country; and second, that it is denied advantages and decencies to which any free country is entitled.'
– Mahatma Gandhi

MOHANDAS GANDHI (1869–1948)

Born in India, Gandhi studied in Britain before working as a lawyer in South Africa, where he helped to make the government repeal laws which were unjust to Indians. After returning to India, his peaceful protests against British rule encouraged rural people to follow his example and eventually force the British to leave. He was known as the Mahatma, or 'great soul', because his simple, honest lifestyle inspired Indians to rebel against their colonial rulers.

To millions of Indians, Mahatma Gandhi was just like them: he dressed and lived very simply. They followed him without question.

15

Measuring development

People often talk about the world's 'rich' and 'poor' countries. Poor countries are often referred to as 'developing', while rich ones have 'developed'.

There are many different ways of measuring how developed a country is. One way is to look at how much wealth a country produces, or its Gross National Product per person (or GNP per capita). This is the wealth created each year by its industries within its borders, plus the money earned from exports, divided by the country's population. The GNP per capita is the amount of money each person in a country would receive if all the wealth was shared equally. Obviously, the bigger a country's GNP, the larger each person's share would be. Rich countries would be able to give their people a lot of money, while poor countries would give theirs a small amount.

The wealth in any country is not shared equally. In India, few people are rich and many, such as this rickshaw puller, are poor.

GROSS NATIONAL PRODUCT PER CAPITA ($)		
Rank		GNP per capita
1	Switzerland	36,080
6	USA	23,240
13	Canada	20,710
16	UK	17,790
17	Australia	17,260
22	New Zealand	12,300
105	China	470
115	India	310
123	Bangladesh	220
132	Mozambique	60

Source: *World Development Report*, World Bank, 1994

Poverty is obvious in much of India. Beggars in cities like Calcutta are often desperate for food.

Switzerland has the highest GNP per person, whereas India ranks 115th, out of 132 countries. In other words, Switzerland is the richest country in the world and India is the eighteenth poorest.

However, a single system such as GNP per capita can be misleading. No country in the world divides its wealth equally between all of its people. There are other ways of working out which are developed and which are developing countries.

According to some experts, for a country to be considered developed:

• there should be no poverty; its people should have the basic necessities of life: food, shelter, clothing, health care and education.

• there should be no unemployment; its people should have jobs to earn money for buying the things they need, and also for their self-respect – to feel that they are contributing something to society.

• there should be no inequality; everyone must be treated justly and fairly, regardless of their background, wealth or sex.

No country can completely wipe out poverty, unemployment and inequality. However, in a developed country these exist on a smaller scale than in a developing nation, where there are many poor people, high unemployment and great inequalities. Like any developing nation, India has its fair share of these three problems.

Even the children who go to school are poorly educated because their schools lack basic facilities such as classrooms, desks and textbooks.

POVERTY IN INDIA

India has some of the poorest people in the world, and not just a few million, but hundreds of millions of them. It has been estimated that 48 per cent of India's population (406 million people) are poor. (In Britain, 18 per cent of the population, or 10 million people, are poor.)

These people's poverty can be measured by the extent to which they are denied many of the basic necessities of daily life, such as clean drinking water, health care and education: the less someone has of these, the poorer he or she tends to be.

Providing them with more basic necessities would give them more opportunities to be better off, not only in terms of having more money, but in having a better life. Not having life's basic necessities is poverty.

For some people, it is difficult even to earn enough money to buy food.

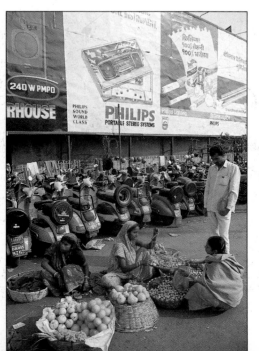

WHO IS POOR IN INDIA?

In the Indian government's eyes, you are 'rich' or 'poor' according to whether you can afford to buy enough food for your minimum daily energy requirements. 'Poor' people cannot afford the minimum number of calories, while 'rich' people can. The government says that country people need to eat a minimum of 2,400 calories and city people 2,100 calories each day. (Country life is tougher, so rural people need more energy.)

18

- 63 per cent of Indian children under 5 years old are malnourished; Bangladesh is the only country in the world where the problem is worse.*
- An Indian woman can expect to live to 62, a man to 61; an American woman to 80 and a man to 73.*
- India has one doctor for 2,460 people; in the USA, there is one doctor for 420 people.*
- In India, there are 1,000 people per hospital bed; in Britain there are 200.**
- 14 per cent of India's population have access to sanitation and 73 per cent to safe water; in most Western countries, everyone has access to santitation and safe water.*
- 52 per cent of Indian adults cannot read and write; in European countries it is less than 5 per cent.*
- In India there is one teacher for every 60 primary school children; in Canada there is one teacher for 15 children.*

Source: * *World Development Report*, World Bank, 1994
** *World Development Report*, 1990

It is difficult for the poor to break out of their poverty. The areas where they live have bad facilities, which means that they have very limited opportunities to better themselves. For example, because there are only a few schools people cannot get a proper education, which means that they cannot get a good job that pays well, so they get stuck where they are.

Unable to satisfy the basic needs of nearly half its population, India itself is a developing country. It cannot begin to think of itself as a developed nation until this level of poverty has been greatly reduced.

With no piped water in their homes, these men are forced to wash on the street.

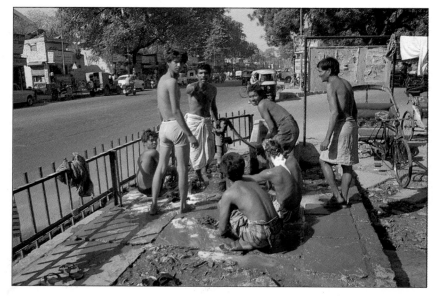

19

Working in India

India does not have enough jobs for all its population. There is a high number of people who are either unemployed, or under-employed. The unemployed have no job whatsoever. Under-employed people have no regular, full-time job. Instead, they do odd jobs, perhaps working only for a few hours a week or for one or two days per week or month.

No one is very sure how many people are unemployed in India. However, after carrying out the population census in 1991, the government estimated it to be 36 million people, or 12.5 per cent of the total work-force.

There are probably the same number of under-employed people. In all, this means that about 72 million people, or 25 per cent of the workforce, are not receiving a proper wage. Assuming that these people have three dependants to support, then a total of 270 million or so persons' lives are affected by a lack of money.

DISTRIBUTION OF THE WORKFORCE		
	India	Britain
Agriculture	62%	2%
Manufacturing industries	11%	20%
Service industries	27%	78%
Source: *World Development Report*, World Bank, 1990		

Many Indians earn some money from part-time work because there are not enough jobs for everyone to work all the time.

As countries develop, it is usual for people to stop working on the land, and to find jobs in factories. In India, more people still work on the land than in industries because there are not enough factory jobs. The reasons for this are partly historical and partly connected with population growth.

FEW FACTORIES

India has few factories, because its industrialization only started after Independence. The British had used India as a source of cheap, agricultural raw materials. Instead of turning India into a nation of factory workers, the British made sure it stayed a nation of farmers. The only factories built in India were for processing crops, ready for shipping them back to Britain. Jute and cotton mills, for example, were constructed to prepare the raw farm crops for the factories at home. Independence from Britain gave India the freedom to start industrializing.

In 1947, industries employed less than 10 per cent of the workforce. Today, they still employ only 11 per cent of the total number of workers.

Most of India's industries are located near the coast, to be close to transport by ship.

N

New Delhi

Bombay

Goa

Bangalore

Madras

Calcutta

○ Steel plant
▼ Oil and Gas
▲ Oil refineries
■ Major port
◆ Major iron ore mine
✳ Petrochemical plant
▽ Space centre
◇ Shipyard
□ Nuclear power station
△ Aircraft manufacture
+++++ Railway

TOO MANY WORKERS

The other reason for India's high unemployment and under-employment is population growth. Although industries have been built quickly, the population has grown even faster. Every day, 70,000 babies are born in India – nearly one per second – and the population has been growing by 2.3 per cent per year, or over 19 million people. (In comparison, the population of Britain increases by 0.2 per cent per year.)

'I didn't want seven children; my husband did. He wanted to impress his friends. He also thought the children would make him rich, but they've only made us poorer. It's so expensive now to educate, feed and clothe them that I've told my eldest daughter to stop at two children, no matter what her husband says.'
– Tulika Kapoor, a mother from Delhi

In India, there are more small workshops, like this one in Calcutta, than factories.

THE IMPORTANCE OF AGRICULTURE

As there are few factories, city jobs are scarce. Most people who go in search of them are disappointed. They end up doing odd jobs and increasing the number of under-employed. The other alternative is to remain in the countryside to work on the land. Agriculture employs 62 per cent of all workers.

A minority make a good living from the land. They are people with large farms in good areas – mainly on the Ganges plain – where they can grow enough for their own needs, and still have a lot of surplus crops to sell for an income.

However, the majority of people in agriculture are either subsistence farmers or labourers, both of whom scratch a living from the land. The subsistence farmers can grow enough to feed themselves, but little or nothing is left over to sell. Many of them farm in areas where the soil is poor and where there is no irrigation during the dry season. They do not have the money to improve their land, and have to do the best they can with their limited resources.

A farmer's wife drying coriander seeds. She is fortunate in having enough land so that some crops can be sold for an income.

THE 'GREEN REVOLUTION' – SUCCESS OR FAILURE?

The Green Revolution is the name given to the changes in agriculture in the last twenty years. The most important one was the introduction of new types of wheat and rice, called high-yielding varieties (HYVs), which increased the size of harvests. However, HYVs required a lot of fertilizers, pesticides and regular watering. Rich farmers could afford to plant HYVs: they had the money to buy the fertilizers and the pesticides and improve their irrigation systems. Poor farmers had to borrow money, which increased their debts. Often, they have not been able to keep on buying the fertilizers and chemicals, so their HYV crops have failed. In much of India, the Green Revolution has only made rich farmers richer and poor farmers even poorer.

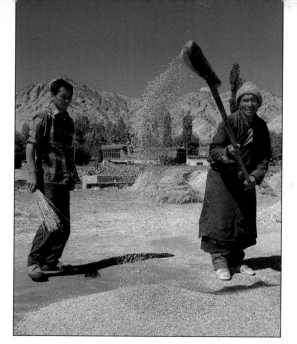

Winnowing the wheat harvest in Ladakh. The soil there is frozen for several months during the cold winters, so nothing can be grown in it and farmers have no work.

Agricultural labourers earn their money from working for farmers, perhaps by helping them to gather the harvest or to sow seeds. Most of their work is seasonal and dependent on the weather. If the monsoon fails or washes away the crops, they get no work. Most agricultural labourers are under-employed.

The 1991 census estimated that 6 per cent of all agricultural male workers were unemployed. However, when the numbers of under-employed were included, this rose to 23 per cent. In 1991, 191 million worked in agriculture, so about 44 million men did not earn full wages.

Even if they had been in full-time work they would have earned little. India's population boom has been most noticeable in the countryside, for this is where the majority of the people live. While the number of rural workers has increased, the amount of land, and therefore the number of jobs, has remained the same. As there are more people wanting work than there are jobs available, wages are low.

Rice, wheat and maize are the main Indian crops.

- Rice
- Forest
- Highland pasture
- Unproductive land
- Arable wheat and maize

MONEY FROM FARMING

Each year the amount of money India earns from agriculture gets smaller. This shrinking sum has to be shared by more and more people, which means that farmers and agricultural labourers are worse off. In fact, recent studies show that they are earning the same as they did in the 1950s. The cost of living today is, of course, much higher.

This Delhi teenager has probably been working for ten years already, to boost his family's income.

For the majority of families, income is more important than education. Many children start working as soon as they can walk and talk.

CHILD LABOUR

The high numbers of unemployed and under-employed adults have caused an increase in the number of children who work since Independence. With their fathers earning little or nothing, the children are used to top up the family income. There are few job opportunities in the their villages, so the children are sent to the nearest town or city, where they do anything offered to them: from pavement shoe cleaning and being the errand boy in a hotel, to jobs in factories or workshops.

Once again, except from the fact that child labour is widespread, no one knows how many children work. However, it seems safe to assume that if an adult replaced every child worker, there would be little unemployment or under-employment in India, and millions would be better off.

'I never went to school so I cannot read or write. I've been working for as long as I can remember. I sell snacks to the people on the Maidan, the huge park in the centre of Calcutta.'
– Arun, aged 13

24

Most employers 'buy' children from parents desperate for money. The employers look upon the children as their slaves, treating them badly, paying them little and making them work long hours in unhealthy conditions. Many children start working at a young age. For example, a recent study of the carpet industry found that 300,000 children were employed in it, 18 per cent (54,000) of whom were under ten years old.

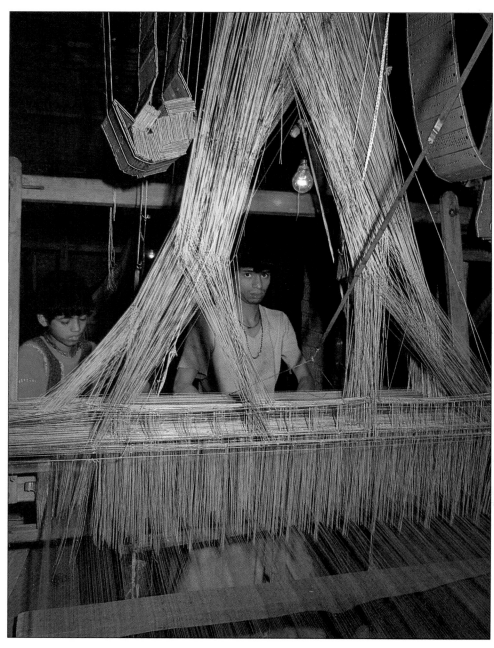

A silk-weaving workshop. Most of the workers in this industry are children, who work in bad conditions for little money.

Street children of Bangalore

Bangalore is the capital of the southern state of Karnataka. It is one of the biggest cities in India, with a population of 3.3 million. Bangalore is the 'Silicon City' of India, full of booming computer and electronics businesses. Space satellites are also made there and launched nearby. These new industries have made Bangalore one of the richest cities in India. Despite this, over 40 per cent of its population lives in slums. Unable to make ends meet, many families have been forced to send their children out to work. Most of them end up on the streets. Here, they are joined by the children who have left home because of family problems brought on by the stresses of slum life and poverty.

There are 45,000 children living and working on Bangalore's streets. About 25,000 of them stay on the streets the whole time, both day and night. Some are orphans with no family to support them. Others have left home because they have been unhappy there. Some of these children keep in contact with their parents, others want nothing to do with them. The remaining 20,000 children work on the streets in the day and return home in the evening with what they have earned.

One of Bangalore's many homeless children keeps warm at night, before curling up to sleep somewhere on the street.

The children who have to go out to earn money work in dark, dusty conditions. They grow up with bad eyesight and breathing problems, which will stop them working. When they become adults, they may be forced to send their

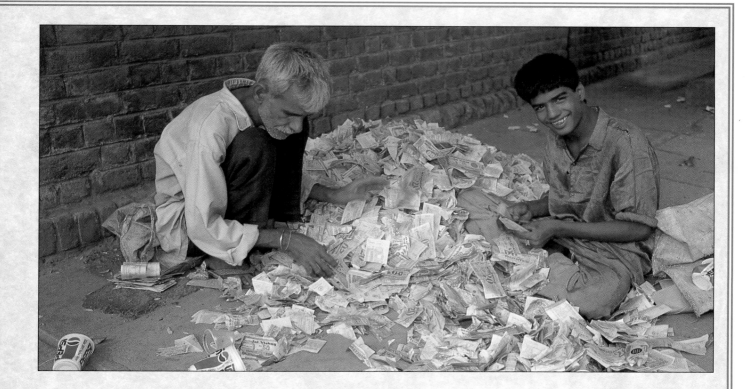

Sorting used lottery tickets before taking them to a recycler, who will sell them to a paper mill.

The ages of the street children range from five or six to late teenagers. About 60 per cent of them are 'rag pickers', who rummage through rubbish for waste, such as paper, plastic or cardboard, for recyclers. In return, the recyclers pay them a few rupees per kilo or give them food and shelter.

Living on the streets brings the children into contact with the criminals of Bangalore. They often tempt the children into theft,

'My parents live in Bangalore. They are drunkards. They used to hit me and shout at me every day. In the end I left home and went to live on the streets. That was six years ago.'
– Padmanabham, aged 16

prostitution or dealing in drugs. The children are constantly harassed by the police and they are sometimes kidnapped by 'slum agents', who force them to work as virtual slaves in factories or hotels.

children out to work. Poverty is the cause of child labour, which causes further poverty and more children being employed to support their families. It is a vicious circle in which millions of Indians are trapped.

Inequalities in society

Although India has become a wealthier country by industrializing, its wealth has not been shared equally between the cities and the countryside. Industries have developed around the cities and it is here that the wealth they have generated has been spent. The countryside has not benefited. For example, the number of country people who can read and write is half the number of people living in the cities. In the villages, nearly twice as many babies die before the first birthday as in the cities. In other words, there are more schools and better health care in the cities than in the countryside, and there are more poor people, and greater poverty, in the countryside.

'We work harder to make up for the money lost by sending two children to school, but it's worth it. My wife and I have suffered because we can neither read nor write. We don't want our children to have the same problems.'
– Jangaiah, farm labourer in Andhra Pradesh state

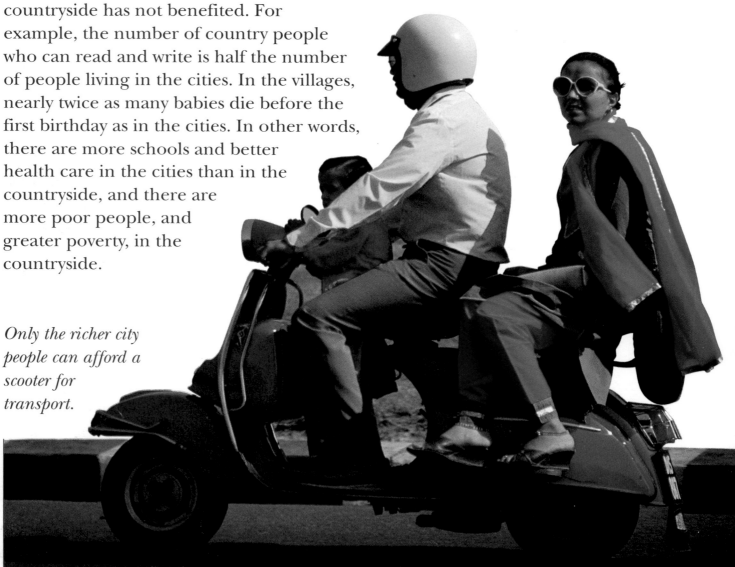

Only the richer city people can afford a scooter for transport.

India is a nation of country people: nearly 75 per cent of the population lives there, in 578,000 villages. The villagers' most important possession is land. It provides them with food, for eating or selling. Cows can be grazed on it to supply milk and dung, which is both a fertilizer and a fuel. Land can be used as security to obtain a loan.

In India, the land is owned unequally: a few people own a lot of it and millions none of it. In between these two groups are the millions of subsistence farmers who own small plots. The British were responsible for this inequality in land ownership. They encouraged the *zemindars* to seize the land of the peasant farmers who could not pay their land tax. The *zemindars* ended up with huge areas of land, which their families still own. Today, it has been estimated that 3 per cent of the population owns 40 per cent of the land. Since Independence, laws have been made to redistribute the land more fairly. However, the laws have not been obeyed and landless people have lacked the confidence to complain.

Most large landowners abuse their powerful positions in rural society. They rent land to landless people in return for a share of the harvests. Frequently, this is an unfair share which leaves the farmers with only just enough to survive on. Other landless people work as labourers for the large landowners, who pay them low wages.

A rich landowner in Gujarat state. Many people who own land have grown wealthy by treating other people unjustly.

People come to the large landowners – who are the richest people in the country – to borrow money. They will be lent it on condition that it is repaid at a high interest rate. Many borrowers fall behind with their repayments and sink further into debt. It is not unusual for the debt to grow so big that it cannot be repaid in the borrower's lifetime, so it is passed on to his children. Whole families can end up in 'bonded labour' to a money-lender, working solely for him until an inherited debt is paid off.

Country people can have a difficult life. If they have no land, they are in the power of greedy landowners. But even if they have their own land, they are still at the mercy of the monsoon. If the rains do not come, or flooding occurs, they may not have enough food. Often, the only way many people can survive is by borrowing from the money-lenders.

Country people try to improve their lives by having many children. In developed countries, large families are seen as a drain on income: the more children you have, the more it will cost you to feed, clothe and educate them. Indians take the opposite view: children can earn money to increase the family income. Many families now rely on their children for incomes. Children can also look after their parents in old age, something that is important in a country where pensions and old people's homes are rare. Because of the low quality of health care in villages, many children die young. In order to ensure that a few of them survive to adulthood, parents have many children.

Most country people think that large families are a help, not a hindrance. This potter's children can help him with his work so that he can earn more money.

TYPICAL MEALS EATEN BY COUNTRY PEOPLE	
Breakfast:	In the north, *paratha* (thick pancake); in the south *idli* (rice dumpling) and a spicy sauce.
Lunch:	Rice, *dhal* (lentil soup), and vegetables, or, in the south, *masala dosa* (stuffed pancake).
Dinner:	Rice, vegetables pulses and *chapatis* (thin pancakes).

While this may help individual families to survive, it worsens the situation for country people as a whole. Already, there are not enough resources for the existing people, so more people will mean that everyone is worse off. For example, land is one of the most scarce resources. The more children in a family, the smaller their share of land on their father's death. The smaller the land, the more difficult it is to grow enough to eat. In the end, a rapidly expanding population threatens the availability of land. It is a country person's most important possession; life is miserable without it.

As India's cities have developed, millions of country people have left the land and moved to them in the hope of having a better, and easier, life there.

CITY LIFE

City life rarely lives up to the hopes of most rural migrants. Once the rural poor, they are now part of the urban poor. They remain on the lowest rung of the social ladder. Even so, few of

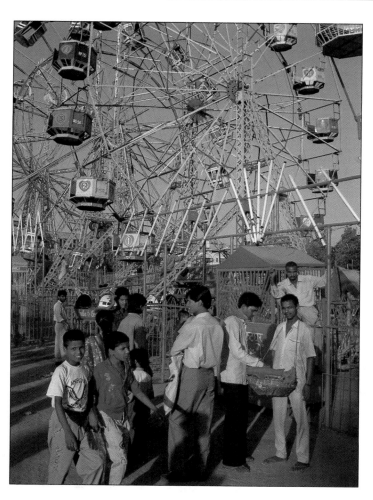

Opportunities for entertainment, as well as work, are more plentiful in cities than in the countryside.

them regret their decision to leave their villages, because they now have access to a wider range of facilities, from basic necessities to leisure activities, such as cinemas and parks. There are also more opportunities to earn an income, especially for landless people. Previously, their jobs had been seasonal and affected by the weather. In the city, the jobs are more regular, come rain or shine.

There are not enough factory jobs for the thousands of rural people who arrive in the cities every day. Most of the migrants end up doing a variety of odd jobs. The industrialization of India has created a wealthy middle class of city business people who require workers in their offices, factories and homes. Employees, too, are needed by the new industries, shops, restaurants and hotels opened to cater for the demands of this new class of people, many of whom have a lot of money to spend. Their incomes equal those of wealthy people in developed countries and they aspire to a similar lifestyle, with designer-label clothes, expensive cars, foreign holidays and all the latest household machines.

Educated and with good jobs, these two city women have lifestyles which country women can only dream about.

THE CASTE SYSTEM

Hindus are divided into four social groups, or castes:
- At the top are the Brahmins, from whom the priests are chosen.
- Next are the Kshatriyas, the soldiers and officials.
- Then come the Vaishyas, the business and crafts people.
- Finally, there are the Sudras, the farmers.

Separate from these castes – literally, 'out-castes' – are the Untouchables, the people with the dirtiest jobs. Today, they prefer to call themselves Dalits, which means 'the oppressed'. They comprise 16 per cent of the population.

Generally, people in the higher castes have the best opportunities in life. For example, 53 per cent of all government officials are Brahmins, even though Brahmins make up only 3 per cent of the population. In the countryside, the upper castes own most of the land, while the lower castes are more often landless.

In country villages, each caste often has its own neighbourhood – with the Dalits living separately – and people marry only within their own caste. In many villages, if a Dalit were to drink from a Brahmin's well, he or she would be stoned to death.

Fuelled by rural migration and the middle class's money, India's cities have exploded in size. Between 1971 and 1981, they grew by 45 per cent; Bangalore alone by 77 per cent. They have reached bursting-point. Public transport groans under the weight of double the number of passengers it was designed to carry; power stations cannot cope with the increased demand for electricity; nor can sewage pipes with the greater amount of waste.

Although they are affected by the problems, the wealthy urban middle class has the resources to cope with them. They have smart homes, cars, servants and generators for their air-conditioners. The urban poor have none of these, so they suffer the most. For example, there is a major shortage of housing in all the cities, which means that homes are very expensive. Unable to afford them, millions of poor people are forced to live on the streets, and in shacks in dirty slums, where diseases spread rapidly in the hot climate. In 1990 the Indian government estimated that 48,800,000 people lived in slums in India, the majority of them in the cities.

A lack of housing means that many village people end up living in filthy city slums, like this one in Delhi.

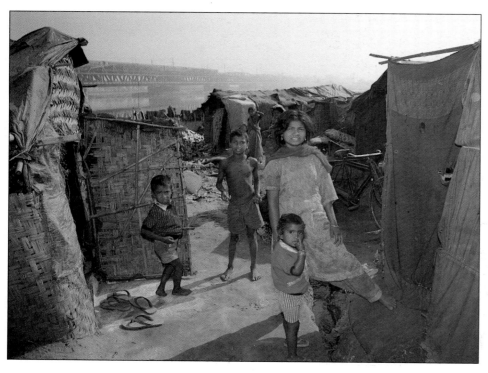

'We thought that city life would be better. We've ended up in a shanty town on the banks of a stinking river full of garbage. We live in a hut made of bits of wood and plastic we've found. It leaks in the rain. There's no electricity and no water, and the children always seem to be sick.'
– Santosh Kumari, hotel porter in Delhi

The Indian government does not have the money to look after this deformed man, so he is forced to beg to survive.

SOCIAL INEQUALITIES

There are many divisions within Indian society which prevent people from improving their lives.

Caste is the biggest barrier to progress. It is very difficult for members of the lowest castes to get a good education and an important job. By law, a percentage of university places and government jobs has to be given to low-caste people. However, putting this into practice has not been easy. Caste is less of a problem in the cities, but in the country it is still a handicap.

Before Independence, Pakistan and Bangladesh were part of India. In 1947 it was decided that India would be a Hindu nation and that the areas where the Muslims lived would become separate Islamic countries. However, many Muslims continued to live in India. Although by law there is no religious discrimination, there is rivalry between the two religions, which often breaks out into violence, and Hindus tend to be given preference over Muslims.

India has traditionally been a male-dominated society. In the cities, there is now more equality between the sexes, but in the countryside the men still make all the important decisions.

RELIGIOUS GROUPS	
	Percentage of population
Hindus	82.6
Muslims	11.3
Christians	2.4
Sikhs	2.0
Buddhists	0.7
Jains	0.5
Others	0.5
Source: *India Book, 1994–95*, D M Silvera	

34

INEQUALITY BETWEEN THE SEXES

India is one of the few countries in the world where there are less women than men. Men are valued more than women because they have traditionally been the income earners, while women have stayed at home. As women usually do not earn money, they are expected to bring some wealth with them when they marry. This is the reasoning behind paying a dowry: that is, the bride's family present her future husband with jewellery, furniture, clothes and, if they are rich, a car or motorbike. Even though dowry payments have been banned by law, many families still expect to receive them.

Parents, whether they are rich or poor, consider daughters a burden because dowry payments usually land them in heavy debt. Often, poor families will not look after a daughter properly and so many girls die young. In the poorest regions of India, some families take more drastic action: they kill their daughters at birth. A booming business in the cities are clinics where a pregnant women can discover the sex of her foetus. If it is female, it will be aborted.

MRS INDIRA GANDHI
Indira Gandhi was the daughter of Jawaharlal Nehru, the first prime minister of Independent India. She also entered politics and became prime minister herself from 1966–77 and 1980–84. Although many of her policies were controversial, she was a strong leader who was devoted to national unity and to the reduction of poverty.

Despite the lowly status of many women, education, wealth and a tough personality all helped Indira Gandhi (bottom right) reach the top in politics.

'Girl killing is also traditional in parts of southern India, particularly in the poor Salem district of Tamil Nadu . . . 51 per cent of families in Salem killed baby girls within a week of their birth to avoid dowry, currently running at around 60,000 rupees – the equivalent of 50 months' wages for an unskilled worker.'
– The Times of India *magazine, 5 March 1994*

Development: improving people's lives

A European doctor helping at health clinic which receives money collected by charities abroad.

Non-governmental organizations (NGOs) are groups of people who have been helping India's poor since British times. The first NGOs were British missionaries and charity workers, who opened churches, schools, hospitals and orphanages. While the poor benefited from their 'good works' in their daily lives, these early NGOs could not halt the number of people who were becoming poor.

In the 1960s, the NGOs decided to adopt a different approach. They thought the solution lay in improving conditions by doing things like digging wells for irrigation and providing better health care. While this was an improvement on the earlier good works, the poor were rarely consulted about what they wanted and little was done to end the social problems which caused poverty. A well may have cured a water problem in a village, but it did nothing to stop a powerful landowner robbing the villagers of their land. The Indian people knew this was the real problem, but they had not been asked about it. A lot of money was wasted on unnecessary projects and the poor continued to grow in numbers.

Providing clean water often helps people to live more easily, but the underlying causes of poverty are often more difficult to solve.

Nowadays it is accepted that the best way to tackle poverty is to ask people about their problems and let them suggest the best ways of solving them. Only in this way can people be helped to help themselves, so that in the future they will not need any outside assistance to lead better lives. This approach also tackles many of the social reasons behind long-term poverty.

Most NGOs in India have concentrated on working in the countryside, where poverty is at its worst. Raising the level of literacy is now considered to be one of the most important ways to improve people's conditions. People without an education are open to all sorts of unjust treatment, which holds back their progress. Money-lenders, for example, can cheat them because they cannot read a loan agreement. Once people can read and write, they are more aware of their rights under the law, which gives them the confidence to challenge people who mistreat them.

As well, educated people are open to new ideas. When mothers attend literacy classes, their children's health also improves, because the teachers often discuss such matters as child care, diet and hygiene. Educated people can learn more easily how to take better care of their children. The chances of their children living to adulthood are much greater, thus reducing the need for such big families.

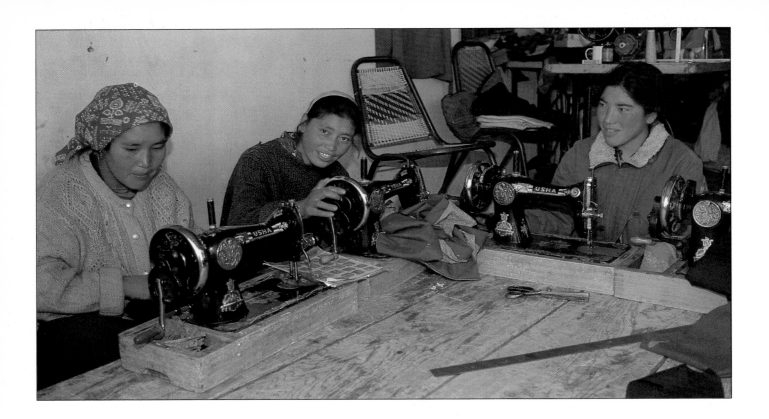

Village women being taught how to use sewing machines so that they can start their own clothes businesses.

'We are being trained to work sewing machines as part of a scheme to increase job opportunities for women. At the end of the course, I can take a sewing machine back to my village. There I will make clothes to sell, as well as train other women to help me.'
– Dolma, from a mountain village in Ladakh

Although it is certainly a bonus, education on its own cannot help landless people to earn a living. If, however, they are taught a skill – perhaps a craft such as weaving or carpentry – they may find regular, better-paid employment. Alternatively it may help to have money to start their own businesses.

NGOs can help with special loans, at low interest rates, so that a newly trained tailor, for example, can buy a sewing-machine without getting into expensive debt with the local money-lender. Farmers, too, can take advantage of these loans to purchase things that will improve their ability to grow food, such as high-yielding varieties of seeds, fertilizers and pesticides, or to dig wells or irrigation channels.

Chembakolli is located in the far south of India. The nearest town is 30 km away, down rough dirt roads. Mysore, the closest city is another 100 km distant.

DEVELOPMENT IN CHEMBAKOLLI

Chembakolli is a remote village among the forested hills in the southern state of Tamil Nadu. It is home to a community of Adivasis, people who are the descendants of the original inhabitants of India. The 51.5 million Adivasis are out-castes, like the Dalits, and live throughout central and southern India. They are mostly subsistence farmers. In Chembakolli they grow rice, onions, tomatoes, peppers and oranges for themselves, plus a little tea and coffee as cash crops.

Rejected by society, the Adivasis are illiterate, own little land and have very limited access to health and education. In the past, their communities have been badly organised, so they have been unable to prevent the government and rich landowners taking away large areas of their land and cutting down the forests. Now, their future is under threat.

Since 1987, an Indian NGO, ACCORD, has been helping the people of Chembakolli to overcome their problems and to fight for their rights. ACCORD has been encouraging the villagers to act together, telling them that they have more power as a group than as individuals. At their regular community meetings, or *sanghams*, the villagers were soon listing all their problems, deciding how urgent each was and taking the appropriate action.

'We know that any problem can be solved because we are a group, not just individuals. We are not afraid any more.'
– Kelu, who regularly attends sanghams in Chembakolli

A sangham in Chembakolli, where people work out how to solve problems that affect them all.

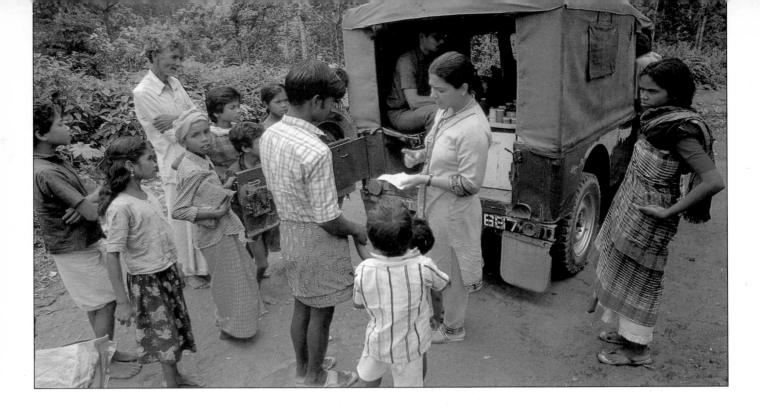

Before doctors visited Chembakolli regularly, people had to walk many miles if they needed medical help.

IMPROVING LIFE IN CHEMBAKOLLI

Money was an issue worrying many people, so ACCORD helped the villagers start a co-operative credit scheme, into which everyone pays two rupees a month. The money is loaned out, for example, to pay off debts to landlords and money-lenders, to buy seeds or to build a house. It is repaid at a very low rate of interest.

The credit scheme is also used to pay two doctors to visit the village regularly. They treat the sick, as well as giving advice on staying healthy. They vaccinate children against polio and measles and hold classes on baby care for pregnant mothers. As a result, fewer babies are dying in their first year and children are living longer. The doctors have also trained health workers in Chembakolli to look after and advise the villagers between their visits.

Buying tea seedlings with the village credit scheme has allowed some people to increase the amount of money they earn.

40

The villagers realized that tea would be a good cash crop, to earn extra money. However, they were short of money to buy the tea seedlings and confused about the ownership of suitable land. The village credit scheme provided the money for the seedlings and ACCORD assisted in sorting out the land-ownership matters.

'Tea used to be the big man's crop. We knew it would be good to grow but we never had enough money for the seeds. Now we have our own land and seeds we can plant in it.'
– Karunakan, who now grows tea on his land

ACCORD has also helped to open a school in Chembakolli. Previously, Adivasi children had gone to local government schools, which they did not enjoy. The children felt very inferior to their upper-caste class mates. The new school is run by villagers who have been trained as teachers by ACCORD. They understand that education is not just about reading, writing and arithmetic: it must make the Adivasi children proud of their culture and confident in their dealings with other Indians, whether Dalits or Brahmins. The teachers also emphasize the need to take care of the environment, for as it deteriorates so do the Adivasi's chances of a better life.

The Adivasi children find it easier to learn at their own school.

'When I was a child, I went to a government school. There was only one other Adivasi child there. We used to wear gold ear-rings, which the other children made fun of. They couldn't understand our language. The teacher told us not to speak it in school, but didn't tell us why. For twelve years I felt that everyone was superior to me.'
– Penchi, who sends his children to the new school

STREET CHILDREN

All of India's street children miss out on education. Living on the streets also affects their health, both physically and mentally. They do not grow as tall as other children because they have a poor diet, sometimes eating food from waste bins. Long after others have grown up, street children are still behaving like children half their age.

Working towards a brighter future

In Bangalore, several NGOs are helping street children to get a better start in life. Several NGOs have opened shelters which are home for some children, while others just visit them during the day. As well, they are helping the children by teaching them skills which will allow them to get jobs. Some shelters give the children food, health advice and classes in carpentry, screen printing, tailoring and electronics.

'On the streets my biggest problem was food; also the police used to arrest me and I had to pay them money to get away. Now I'm in [a] shelter and I wear decent clothes, eat and wash every day. My lessons are also helping me to start planning for the future. None of this would have happened a few years ago.'
– Bijl, aged 10

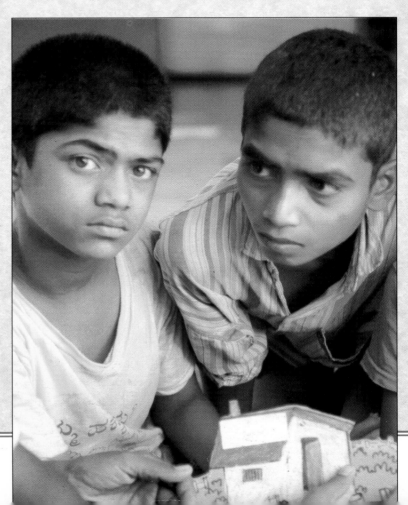

Bijl, on the left, now has hope for a better future since he began going to the shelter.

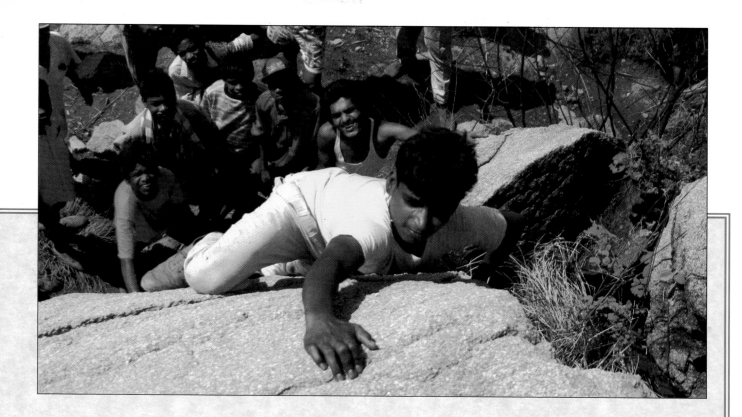

Outdoor pursuits also help to give the shelter's children the confidence to cope with challenging situations.

Children over 16 can go to another NGO after they have learnt a skill. The staff try to find them jobs with local firms, most of whom are usually reluctant to employ ex-street children. To make it easier for them to get employed, the teenagers are

'Local employers want responsible, reliable, honest workers – qualities they don't think street children have. My job is to convince them that they're wrong. You can find these qualities in our teenagers.'
– Solomon Jayaprakash, who works in a shelter

'I've been working as a garage mechanic for one year. It's a great job and I would like to open my own business one day. Without help, I'd still be a rag picker, and I never want to go back to that.'
– Lokech, one of the shelters' success stories

taught the skills they need to keep a full-time job. There is also an effort to build up their self-confidence with outdoor activities, such as rock-climbing, which encourage them to tackle difficult tasks.

India tomorrow

Many tourists visit India. The money they bring into the country is an important source of income.

Cut off by the high Himalayas, Ladakh has missed out on India's post-Independence prosperity.

There is no doubt that India made a great leap forward since Independence. In 1947 only 15 per cent of adults could read and write; few could expect to live beyond their late twenties; there were frequent food shortages; hardly any villages had electricity; and there was very little industry. Even so, despite the progress, today India has twice as many poor people as neighbouring China, which has a bigger population.

Mahatma Gandhi believed that poverty could be reduced if India concentrated on improving conditions in the countryside. As the countryside prospered, Gandhi said, it would push the rest of India forward: India would develop from the bottom up.

Jawaharlal Nehru, Independent India's first prime minister, believed the opposite: India should advance from the top down. Nehru gave priority to heavy' industries in the belief that they would pull India forward, with all Indians benefiting from the progress.

Will the wealth created by India's new industries 'trickle down' to these street sellers?

Today, the government continues to follow Nehru's line of thinking. It considers that the wealth created by the rich people at the top will trickle down to the poor below them. The government anticipates that the richer the middle class becomes, the more it will buy. Then, more factories will have to be built and more jobs will become available for the poor. If this happens, all India's people will be better off.

Even if this plan works, it will be many years before there are any noticeable benefits. Until then, India's poor will need to be supported so that they are in a better position to improve their own lives.

FOREIGN DEBT

To help pay for India's industrialization, the government has had to borrow money. In 1992 the World Bank said India owed a total of $72 billion, which will rise to $92 billion by 1997. Every year, India has to use 13 per cent of its earnings from exports to repay this debt. The further into debt India gets, the more difficult it is for it to help its own people.
Source: *World Development Report*, World Bank, 1994

Glossary

Alluvium Earth or sand left behind by flood or river waters.

Astronomy Study of the sun, moon, planets and stars in the sky.

Calorie A unit of energy produced by food.

Census An government count of all the people in a country.

Colonialism When a country is controlled by another country that is usually richer and more powerful. The controlled country becomes a colony.

Deforestation Cutting down large areas of forest.

Debt Owing money to another person or country.

Dependant Someone, such as a wife or child, who depends on another person to earn money.

Famine Not having enough food for anyone to eat.

Fertilizer Something added to the soil to make it better for growing crops.

Gross National Product (GNP) The money a country earns within its borders, plus money from exports.

Illiterate Being unable to read or write; signs of a poor education.

Independence When a colony becomes free from foreign rule.

Indigo A blue dye, for dying cloth such as cotton, obtained from a plant.

Interest rate The money that has to be repaid regularly to pay for money that has been borrowed.

Irrigation Adding water to land to grow crops when it would otherwise be too dry.

Jute A fibre obtained from the bark of a plant, used to make sacks and mats.

Life expectancy The number of years a person can expect to live.

Literacy Being able to read and write.

Loan Money that has been borrowed.

Malnourished Not having enough food to eat.

Migrant A person who has moved from home to live in another town or country.

Monsoon The name of the wind that brings the summer rain; the rainy season, too, is often referred to as 'the monsoon'.

Overgrazing Allowing animals on pasture to eat too much, so that the land becomes bare. This often leads to soil erosion.

Pesticides Chemicals used to kill insects, to stop them from eating and destroying crops.

Raw materials Materials in their natural state, such as coal, iron ore.

Recycling Turning rubbish and waste into something that can be re-used.

Sanitation Drains and pipes for removing waste.

Service industries Industries, such as tourism and banking, which do not make goods, but supply people with services they need.

Soil erosion The wearing away of the soil by wind or rain.

Subsistence Growing food or earning money that is just enough to live on.

Tourist Person from a different country who is on holiday.

Zemindars Large landowners, who became powerful under British rule.

Further information

The Development Education Association can provide the address of local resource centres in Britain carrying materials about India and development.
3rd Floor, Cowper Street, London EC2A 4AP

Many of the NGOs working in India provide a wide range of material on India, including wall charts, teaching packs and videos for loan:
ActionAid: Hamlyn House, Archway, London N19 5PG. Tel: 0171 282 4101.
Christian Aid: P O Box 100, London SE1 7RT. Tel: 0171 60 4444.
Oxfam: 274 Banbury Road, Oxford OX2 7D. Tel: 0865 56777.
Save the Children Fund: Mary Datchelor House, 17 Grove Lane, London SE5 8RD. Tel: 0171 703 5400.
Unicef: 55–6 Lincoln's Inn Fields, London WC2A 3NB. Tel: 0171 405 5592.

Books to read

Countries of the World: India by David Cumming, Wayland, 1989
Hinduism by Hemant Kanitar, Wayland, 1985
Mahatma Gandhi by Michael Nicholson, Exley, 1987
The Partition of India by Hemant Kanitar, Wayland, 1987
The Ganges by David Cumming, Wayland, 1993

For more advanced readers
Chasing the Monsoon by Alexander Frater, Penguin, 1991
No Full Stops in India by Mark Tully, Penguin, 1992

Films

Gandhi A dramatization of the life of India's most famous leader. Available on video.
Salaam Bombay A realistic portrayal of street children in Bombay.
Heat and Dust Contrasting stories of a woman living in 1920s colonial India, and her great-niece who arrives there 60 years later. Available on video.

Index

Numbers in **bold** refer to illustrations.

What is a fraction?

A fraction is part of a whole. The word 'fraction' comes from the Latin word 'fractio', meaning to break. A fraction is one number that has been broken up by another.

1/2
1/4
1/8
1/16

A fraction is written using two numbers. The top number, called the numerator, is the number of pieces we have. The bottom number, called the denominator, is the number of pieces in the whole.

numerator

3/8

denominator

FRACTION
FRENZY

Fractions,
decimals and
combinations

Rob Colson

Acknowledgments and Picture credits

Published in Great Britain in 2018
by The Watts Publishing Group

Copyright © The Watts Publishing Group, 2016

All rights reserved.

Series editor: Sarah Peutrill

Produced by Tall Tree Ltd
Design: Ben Ruocco
Consultants: Hilary Koll and Steve Mills

Every attempt has been made to clear copyright. Should there be any inadvertent omission please apply to the publisher for rectification.

ISBN: 978 1 4451 4946 2

Printed in China

Franklin Watts
An imprint of
Hachette Children's Group
Part of The Watts Publishing Group
Carmelite House
50 Victoria Embankment
London EC4Y 0DZ

An Hachette UK Company
www.hachette.co.uk

www.franklinwatts.co.uk

Picture credits:
t-top, b-bottom, l-left, r-right, c-centre, front cover-fc, back cover-bc
All images courtesy of Dreamstime.com, unless indicated:
Inside front Jefunne; fc, bc Pablo631; fctr Mycoolsites; fcc Artigiano; fcbl Kakigori; 1c, 22b Peter Bertok; 4, 28b Burlesck; 5b Skripko Ievgen; 5b Ahmet Ihsan Ariturk; 6t, 22tl Photka; 7br Maxim Popov; 8t Mirko Milutinovic; 8br, 31tr Cjansuebsri; 9c Aremac; 9cr Wuka; 9bl Stefanschurr226; 9br Franz Pfluegl; 10l Kmiragaya; 11tr Nakedcm; 11c, 29tr Macrolink; 11b, 23b Mexrix; 11br Hvat10; 12b Chaoss; 13c Winnond; 13bl Jordygraph; bctr, 14br Ronstik; 15t Vectorverde; 15bl Szefei; fccl, 16b Liligraphie; bccr, 17tr Matriyoshka; 19b Luislouro; fcbr, 20l Mikkel Strøbech; fccr, 20tl Martin Malchev; fcc, 20tc Shaeree Mukherjee; 23b Stoupa; 23br NASA; bctl, 24-25t Katrina Brown; bctl, 24-25t Wolfgangbeyer; 25br Oleksandr Solonenko; 27 Andreadonetti; 29b Luanateutzi; fctc, 30t Fotosv; 30b Alexmoe; 32t Stylephotographs

Equivalent fractions are different ways to express the same size:

$$^8/_{16} = {^4/_8} = {^2/_4} = {^1/_2}$$

8/16

4/8

2/4

1/2

Improper fractions

Improper fractions represent more than a whole, so, for instance $^5/_4$ is **five quarters**, which can be arranged to make **1** and $^1/_4$.

Ancient fractions

The ancient Romans wrote fractions using multiples of twelfths: such as $^1/_{12}$, $^1/_{24}$ or $^1/_{144}$. They would think of $^1/_2$ as **six twelfths**, and it was called a **semi**. The ancient Babylonians wrote fractions as the number of sixtieths, so $^1/_2$ would be **30 sixtieths**.

The first people to write out fractions using a numerator and a denominator were the Indians in around 500 CE. Later, Arab scholars added a line between the two. This system was flexible as you could use any number as the denominator.

Sums with fractions

Adding fractions

Adding fractions with the same denominator is easy.

$$1/6 + 3/6 = 4/6$$

Where the denominators are different, you first need to find a common denominator. The simplest way to do this is to multiply the denominators together.

(Numerator A) x (Denominator B)
1 x 6

(Numerator B) x (Denominator A)
1 x 5

$$1/5 + 1/6 = 6/30 + 5/30 = 11/30$$

Ⓐ Ⓑ

5 x 6

(Denominator A) x (Denominator B)

Often the answer can be simplified. For instance,

$$3/8 + 1/6 = 18/48 + 8/48 = 26/48$$

$$13/24$$

dividing both numerator and denominator by **2** gives
so **24** is the **lowest common denominator**

Subtraction

Subtracting fractions is very similar
to addition. Find a common denominator
and subtract one numerator from the other:

(2 x 4)   (1 x 5)

$$2/5 - 1/4 = 8 - 5/20$$

$$= 3/20$$

(5 x 4)

Multiplying

Multiplying fractions can be summed up as: $\dfrac{\text{Top times top over}}{\text{Bottom times bottom}}$

so, $3/5 \times 7/9 = (3 \times 7)/(5 \times 9) = 21/45$

You may need to simplify to find the **lowest denominator**.
In this instance, you can divide both numerator
and denominator by **3**:

$$21/45 = 7/15$$

Division

Division is almost as easy as multiplication: Turn
the second fraction upside down and multiply, so:

$$2/5 \div 3/4 = 2/5 \times 4/3 = (2 \times 4)/(5 \times 3) = 8/15$$

$4/3$ is called the **reciprocal** of $3/4$. $3/4 \times 4/3 = 12/12 = 1$
Any number **multiplied** by its
reciprocal **equals 1**.

Pete is looking to set up a market
stall selling fruit and veg, but he's not
sure whether it is worth it.

He must give $1/3$ of his takings to
the supplier and then a further
$1/4$ to pay rent for the market stall.

**After paying his expenses,
what fraction of his takings
are left as profit?**

To work out how much of the takings Pete
will have in profit, take his expenses away
from 1. This gives:
$1 - 1/3 - 1/4$

Find a common denominator by multiplying
3 x 4 = 12. That makes:
$12/12 - 4/12 - 3/12 = 5/12$
So Pete will keep $5/12$ of the takings in profit.

"Roll up,
everything is
$1/2$ price!"

7

Fractions to decimals

A decimal is a way of writing down a number in base 10. Each digit in a decimal number represents a multiple or fraction of ten.

Decimal point

| Hundreds 100s | Tens 10s | Units | Tenths 1/10 | Hundredths 1/100 |

The **decimal point** shows the space between the whole units and the tenths. A decimal fraction is a fraction with a denominator that is a **multiple of ten**:
$$^6/_{10} = 0.6, \ ^{43}/_{100} = 0.43, \ ^{125}/_{1000} = 0.125$$

To convert a fraction to a decimal, you first need to find an equivalent fraction with a denominator that is a multiple of 10. For instance,
$$^1/_5 = \ ^2/_{10} = 0.2, \ ^1/_4 = \ ^{25}/_{100} = 0.25$$
Sometimes, you cannot make an exact decimal from a fraction. For instance, converting $^1/_3$ to a decimal produces 0.333..., where **...** means **'recurring'**. This means that the **3s go on for ever**.
Other recurring decimals include:
$$^1/_9 = 0.111... \text{ (1 repeating)},$$
$$^1/_{11} = 0.090909... \text{ (09 repeating)}$$

Calculators use decimal fractions. At some point, the calculator needs to **round** a recurring decimal to the nearest decimal place. This means that you round the last digit **down** if the next digit is **under 5**, and **up** if the next digit is **5 or more**. For instance, to five decimal places $^1/_3 = 0.33333$, while $^1/_{11} = 0.09091$

0.333333

Stop the clock!

Sprint races, like the 100m are timed to the nearest

1/100

(0.01) of a second. The starter fires the starter gun to start the race. This sends an electric signal to start the timer. At the finish line, a high-speed camera pointing straight across the line captures the moment when the athletes cross it. Some part of the torso must cross the line to count as having finished, stopping the clock.

A composite photo shows all the finishers in a 100 metre race. The lines show the moment they stopped the clock.

9.96 seconds

10.23 seconds

9.85 seconds

10.08 seconds

10.29 seconds

10.13 seconds

9.91 seconds

10.06 seconds

10.4   10.3   10.2   10.1   10.0   9.9   9.8

False start

Pressure-sensitive starting blocks sense when the athletes start to move. A false start is recorded if any athlete moves before the gun or up to 0.1 ($1/10$) seconds after the gun.

Starting block

Bang of gun

Signal from brain to legs

Sound to ear

Scientists have calculated that nobody can hear the sound of the gun and send signals to their muscles in less than this time, so if an athlete moves, say, 0.05 ($5/100$) seconds after the gun, they must have anticipated the start before the gun sounded.

Egyptian fractions

The ancient Egyptians wrote out every fraction as a sum of fractions with a numerator of 1. These are called reciprocals, or unit fractions, and the Egyptians wrote them like this.

$$\bigcirc\!\!\!-\!\!\!\bigcirc = 1/2$$

$$2 = 1/2$$

$$3 = 1/3$$

$$5 = 1/5$$

Each fraction in the series to be summed had to be different. So, for instance,

$2/3$ could not be $1/3 + 1/3$

Rather:

$$2/3 = 1/2 + 1/6 \text{ or}$$
$$2/3 = 1/3 + 1/4 + 1/12$$

or you could make a really long series like this:

$$2/3 = 1/4 + 1/7 + 1/12 +$$
$$1/13 + 1/21 + 1/31 + 1/42$$
$$+ 1/156 + 1/420 + 1/930$$

In fact, for every fraction, there is an infinite number of different Egyptian fraction series!

Egyptian fractions are very useful when working out fair shares, and the Egyptians used them to divide their bread rations.

"Hey, hands off."

For instance, if you have eight workers but just five loaves, **how do you divide the bread equally** among your workers? You could slice each of the five loaves into eight pieces. The workers would get five slices each. However, using Egyptian fractions can give you a better solution:

$$5/8 = 1/2 + 1/8$$

So you slice one loaf into eight and the other four into half. Each worker gets two pieces — $1/2$ and $1/8$. Less slicing and fewer crumbs than five $1/8$s!

Smart thinking

Old Josiah the stable keeper has three children, Agnes, Jake and Patrick. He has 12 prize horses, and he decides in his will to leave $1/2$ of his horses to Agnes, $1/3$ to Jake and $1/12$ to Patrick. However, Old Josiah dies in a riding accident that also kills one of his horses, leaving just 11 to be inherited. Patrick is only to be left $1/12$ of the horses, which is just $11/12$ of a horse!

How could they solve their problem?

Old Josiah's lawyer Frances comes up with the solution. She adds her own horse to the prize horses to make them back up to 12. Now the inheritance can be decided exactly:

Agnes gets $1/2 \times 12 = 6$ horses
Jake gets $1/3 \times 12 = 4$ horses
Patrick gets $1/12 \times 12 = 1$ horse

That's a total of 11 horses, so Frances takes her horse back home with her and everyone is happy. It turns out that when he was writing his will, Old Josiah had got his sums slightly wrong: $1/2 + 1/3 + 1/12 = 11/12$, not $12/12$.

Irrational numbers

What is the square root of 2?

In the sixth century BCE, a group of Greek mathematicians called the Pythagoreans thought they had discovered a beautiful idea. Everything in the Universe, they believed, could be described by whole numbers, either on their own or combined to make fractions. Their motto was

"All is number".

The group's leader, Pythagoras, has given his name to one of the most famous proofs in maths: In a **right-angled triangle**, the square of the hypotenuse **equals the sum** of **the squares** of the other two sides.

$$c^2$$

$$a^2$$

$$a \quad c$$

$$b$$

$$b^2$$

$$a^2 + b^2 = c^2$$

? 1

1

One of Pythagoras's followers, Hippasus, asked the question: **What about a square with sides 1 unit long? What is the length of its diagonal?**

According to Pythagoras's theorem, the **length of the diagonal** equals **√2** – that's a number that, **multiplied by itself**, makes 2. It's a number between 1 and 2, but this was no problem for the Pythagoreans as long as they could write the **improper fraction** in the form a/b, **where a and b are whole numbers**. The problem was that Hippasus proved that you cannot do that.

There are no values a and b for which **$a/b \times a/b = 2$**

Legend has it that the unfortunate Hippasus was drowned at sea because of his disturbing discovery. But he had made a huge contribution to mathematics – he had discovered irrational numbers, which are all the numbers that we cannot write as a/b.

diameter

circumference

Irrationally useful

It turns out that many of the most important numbers in maths are irrational.

Pi (π) is the **ratio** of a circle's **circumference** to its **diameter**.

pi = 3.14159...

The number **e** is used in many branches of maths. Known as the **exponential number**, it describes a phenomenon called exponential growth, in which the rate of growth increases as size increases.

e = 2.71828...

1

1.61803...

The Golden Ratio, **phi (φ)**, describes a **rectangle** in which the ratio between both its sides added together and its longer side is **equal** to the ratio between the longer side and the shorter side.

phi = 1.61803...

Cracking combinations

While fractions break wholes into pieces, combinations put pieces together. The branch of maths that deals with combinations is called combinatorics. We use this maths to keep our secrets safe.

How secure is your lock?

On a combination lock using numbers, working out how many different combinations there are is reasonably easy. With four numbers, each from **0 to 9**, you have

10 different numbers for each position, so there are

10 x 10 x 10 x 10 combinations, from

0000 to 9999. That's

10,000 combinations

Each extra digit added to the lock multiplies the number of combinations by 10, so adding one digit makes the lock **10 times harder to crack**.

PASSWORD

When choosing a password for an internet site, there is a choice between letters, digits or symbols for each character. There are **26 letters** that can be upper or lower case, **10 digits** and around **33 other symbols**. That makes

26 + 26 + 10 + 33 = 95

This means that for an eight-character password, there are

95 x 95 x 95 x 95 x 95 x 95 x 95 x 95 = 95^8 = 6.6 quadrillion possibilities

(1 quadrillion = 1,000 billion)

To make a secure password, you should choose a mix of characters at random. However, most of us choose passwords that we find memorable. The most popular eight-character password on the internet is **'password'**. The second most popular is **'12345678'**. Other popular passwords include **'baseball'**, **'football'** and pet names. Hackers make lists of popular combinations and try them out using computer programs, so to be safe, you will need to come up with something much more random. For instance, the password below may be hard to remember, but it would also be impossible to guess:

4H_@jr8Q

A password of Fudge2009 might be cracked by a hacker if your dog is called Fudge, her birth year is 2009 and you posted pictures of her as a puppy on your social media page.

Secret codes

Sending secret messages is called cryptography. A code is used to substitute one letter for another, and you make sense of the message by applying the code in reverse. For instance, what might the code below mean?

OJKNZXMZO

Here, the code is a simple one: arrange all the letters in a line and move back five letters for each letter. When you reach A, go back to Z. Reversing the process to undo the code, you need to add five letters:

TOPSECRET

This is called a substitution cipher, in which one letter is substituted for another according to a mathematical rule. In ancient Rome, Julius Caesar used this substitution cypher to keep his messages secret.

You can make your own codes using whatever rules you like. As long as both you and the recipient of the message know the cypher, they will be able to read it.

Factorisation

Banks employ a far more secure form of encryption to protect their customers' money, using prime factorisation. Prime factorisation is the breaking down of a number into its prime factors. These are numbers that can only be divided by 1 and themselves. Factorising small numbers is easy. For instance,

$$15 = 3 \times 5$$
$$26 = 2 \times 13$$
$$84 = 2 \times 2 \times 3 \times 7$$
$$105 = 3 \times 5 \times 7$$

It is easy to make a large number out of its prime factors. For instance,

$2 \times 2 \times 3 \times 5 \times 11 \times 13 \times 17 \times 31 \times 79 \times 97$
$= 34{,}649{,}480{,}580$

However, there is no easy way to work backwards. Without knowing the answer, it takes a lot of computer power to factorise **34,649,480,580**. It is easy to make a number by multiplying primes that are 30 digits long, but it would take a computer billions of years of calculating to factorise it. Codes built by making large numbers out of prime factors are effectively unbreakable.

"You've got no chance mate."

An Enigma machine

Cracking the Enigma code

During World War II (1939–45), the German army used a device called the Enigma machine to send secret radio messages. It used a combination of electrical wires and rotors to encode messages with 158,962,555,217,826,360,000 (nearly 159 quintillion) possible combinations.

British codebreakers found repeated patterns in the Enigma messages that reduced the possible combinations down to a more manageable 100,000. They constructed a huge calculating machine, called the Bombe, which could work through combinations mechanically. Teams of workers put radio messages through the Bombe, and eventually they broke the code. The codebreakers worked at Bletchley Park, where they were led by the brilliant mathematician Alan Turing. Their role in helping to end the war remained a secret for many decades.

Numbers going bang!

To work out combinations of objects where we can only use each object once, we need an operation called a factorial.

In a classroom with **6 desks** and **6 pupils**, how many different ways can the pupils arrange themselves? Looking at each desk in turn, there are **6 choices** for the first desk. Once the first desk is taken, there are then **5 pupils** and **5 desks** left, so for each of the 6 choices for the first desk, there are 5 choices for the **second desk**. With the second desk filled, there are **4 choices** for the **third desk**, and so on all the way down to the last desk. The number of possible combinations is:

$$6 \times 5 \times 4 \times 3 \times 2 \times 1 = 720$$

This is written as 6! or 6 factorial, sometimes called 6 bang.

It would take a while, but eventually you could try out all **720 combinations** with **six desks**. But what about a larger classroom with **24 desks**?

Factorials get big very quickly, and you often need a calculator to work them out. If you have **24 desks** and **24 pupils**, the number of possible arrangements is

$$24! = 620,448,401,733,239,439,360,000$$

If you had been trying one million combinations per second ever since the start of the Universe, you would still be nowhere near getting through them all!

Dividing one factorial by another is not so difficult. For instance,

$$\frac{6!}{4!} = \frac{6 \times 5 \times \cancel{4} \times \cancel{3} \times \cancel{2} \times \cancel{1}}{\cancel{4} \times \cancel{3} \times \cancel{2} \times \cancel{1}}$$

That leaves $6 \times 5 = 30$. But what about big numbers? What is the value of

$$\frac{15!}{13!}$$

Luckily you don't have to write it out in full:

$$\frac{15 \times 14 \times 13 \times 12 \times 11 \ldots \times 1}{13 \times 12 \times 11 \ldots \times 1}$$
$$=$$
$$\frac{15 \times 14 \times 13!}{13!}$$

so that leaves

$$15 \times 14 = 210$$

And we did all that without ever working out the values of either 15! or 13!

Multiplying factorials

Multiplying factorials is a little tricky, but you only need to find the value of the smaller factorial. For instance, what is the value of **8! × 6!?** Rewrite **8!** as **(8 × 7 × 6!)**. This gives:

$$8! \times 6! =$$
$$8 \times 7 \times 6! \times 6! =$$
$$8 \times 7 \times 720 \times 720$$
$$= 29{,}030{,}400$$

"I don't like sitting here."

Achilles and the tortoise

In the fifth century BCE, the Greek philosopher **Zeno of Elea** posed a series of mathematical brainteasers, now known as Zeno's paradoxes. The most famous involved a hypothetical race between the great warrior and athlete Achilles and a tortoise.

In a race over **10 metres**, Achilles gives the tortoise a 2-metre head start. But Achilles runs at **2 metres per second**, while the tortoise moves at just **1 metre per second**, so surely Achilles will win easily. Zeno suggests that Achilles can never catch the tortoise.

He reasons as follows:
▶ After **1 second**, Achilles will have run **2 metres**. In that time, the tortoise will have moved **1 metre**, so it will be **1 metre ahead**.
▶ Achilles takes **1/2 second** to move this **1 metre**, in which time the tortoise will be **1/2 metre** ahead.
▶ Achilles takes **1/4 second** to move this **1/2 metre**, by which time the tortoise will be **1/4 metre** ahead.

START

After 5 seconds

After 2 seconds

After 1 second

1   2   3

These distances form a series of numbers, each of which is
half the value of the number before it:

$$2 + 1 + \frac{1}{2} + \frac{1}{4} + \frac{1}{8} + \frac{1}{16} + \ldots$$

As this series goes on into infinity, it approaches, but never reaches, 4.
In Zeno's words:

**"In a race, the quicker runner can never overtake
the slower, since the chaser must first reach the point
from which the chased started, so that the slower
must always hold a lead."**

Solving the paradox

A paradox is something that appears logical, but that
we know cannot possibly be correct. Zeno's logic seems sound,
but it just can't be right. The time periods being considered
are also **halving in length** each time:

$$1 + \frac{1}{2} + \frac{1}{4} + \frac{1}{8} + \frac{1}{16} + \ldots$$

This series approaches, but never reaches, 2. But time doesn't stop.
It will click over to 2 seconds, at which point, Achilles and the tortoise
will be **level at 4 metres**. As time clicks on, Achilles will cross the
finishing line after **5 seconds**. After 5 seconds, the tortoise will be
3 metres from the line. Achilles will win easily.

One possible solution to Zeno's paradox of Achilles and the tortoise comes
from physics. There may be a **minimum length of time** that can be
counted and a **minimum length of space** that can be measured. It may
be that, in reality, as opposed to maths, things cannot be divided for ever. At
some point, the series will come to an end, we will reach the **smallest time**
and **length possible**, and Achilles will catch the tortoise.

FINISH

4   5   6   7   8   9

METRES

Fractals

A fractal is a special kind of self-repeating pattern that looks like the same pattern up-close as it does from far away.

Sierpinski triangle

The Sierpinski triangle is a simple fractal that you can draw for yourself.

▶ **Step 1** Start with an equilateral triangle with a solid colour.

▶ **Step 2** Draw another triangle by connecting the mid-points of each side of your triangle, and remove the colour from this triangle.

▶ **Step 3** Repeat the same process for each of the three smaller triangles.

▶ **Steps 4, 5, etc.** Repeat the process again and again...

The triangle contains a number of fraction series.
After Step 2, the fraction of the triangle that is left is $3/4$
After Step 3, the fraction left is $9/16$
After Step 4, the fraction left is $27/64$
After Step 5, the fraction left is $81/256$
Each time, the fraction is the square of the fraction before it:
$$9/16 = 3^2/4^2, \quad 27/64 = 3^3/4^3, \quad 81/256 = 3^4/4^4$$
Can you see why this is?

Step 1

Step 2

Step 3

Step 4

This pattern can also be made in three dimensions to give a Sierpinski pyramid.

A fractal snowflake

Snowflakes are among the many fractal patterns seen in nature.
Here's how to make a six-pointed snowflake fractal.

▶ **Step 1** Start with an equilateral triangle.
▶ **Step 2** Divide each side of the triangle into three equal parts. From each end of the central parts, draw two lines of equal length to make equilateral triangles.
▶ **Step 3 and 4** Now repeat this same process for each side of your new shape. And repeat again and again.

Step 1

Step 2

Step 3

Step 4

Nature's fractals

Self-repeating fractal shapes are found all around us. The shape of a tree is a fractal, with branches coming from the trunk, attached to smaller and smaller branches and twigs. Clouds are fractal patterns, which makes it hard for us to tell how far away from us they are.

Coastlines are fractals. This is the coastline at the Nile Delta in Egypt.

Here is the Mandlebrot set at four different levels of magnification.

Mandlebrot set zoomed out

Zooming in on a circle, you start to see the heads and shoulders of the set

Mandlebrot magic

In the 1970s, the Belgian mathematician Benoit Mandlebrot discovered an extraordinary mathematical set based on a very simple mathematical formula. It uses numbers called complex numbers, which include the square root of -1.

To draw the Mandlebrot set as a graph, a computer tests each value near the edge of the set to see whether or not it lies **inside** or **outside** the set. It then adds a point to the graph. The exact edge can never be worked out precisely, but the **more times** the computer tests the points at the edge, **the finer the detail** of the set becomes.

Zooming in ever closer to the edge of the set reveals self-repeating patterns of extraordinary complexity.

Zooming in on the edge, you find intricate
sea horse tails appear

Zoom in even closer, and the original pattern
starts to re-emerge

Fractal geometry

Mandlebrot's work gave rise to a new branch
of mathematics known as fractal geometry.
Fractals are used to create computer
graphics, to understand earthquakes,
and even to predict changes
in the stock market.

This is a
fractal pattern,
and the patterns
never repeat each
other exactly.
Colours are added
to show how many
times it takes to
test each point.

Romanesco
broccoli has a fractal
geometry of spirals
that looks like
parts of the
Mandlebrot set.

25

Fooled by a fraction

The extra square

The shape above is made up of the following pieces:

A triangle with height 3 and base 8 (red)
A triangle with height 2 and base 5 (green)
Two L-shapes – one made up of rows of 5 and 3 (blue), and the other with rows of 5 and 2 (yellow)

When you rearrange the shapes so that the **small triangle** is at the bottom, a hole appears as if by magic! **Where has the hole come from?**

The answer is that you have been **tricked**. The red and green triangles are not similar – the red triangle has a height-to-base **ratio of $^3/_8$**, while the green has a **ratio of $^2/_5$**. Finding the common denominator, the ratios are **red $^{15}/_{40}$** and **green $^{16}/_{40}$**, meaning that the slope of the green triangle is steeper than the slope of the red triangle. The shapes you have made are not quite triangles. Check with a ruler to be sure.

The smallest fraction ever?

Whatever number you can think of, you can always add 1 to make a bigger number. This means that there are infinite numbers. Infinity is represented in maths by the symbol "∞". Similarly, whatever fraction you can think of, you can always make a smaller fraction – $1/\infty$. This is known as an **infinitesimal**, and it is smaller than the smallest number you can think of.

Infinitesimals do not behave like normal fractions. In fact, there is a mathematical proof that $1/\infty = 0$. Here's how it works: The number $1 - 1/\infty = 0.999...$ (that's 0.999 recurring, with the 9s going on for ever). See if you can follow it! First, let

$$x = 0.999...$$

Multiply both sides by 10:

$$10x = 9.999...$$

This can also be written as:

$$10x = 9 + 0.999...$$

That's the same as:

$$10x = 9 + x$$

Subtract x from both sides:

$$9x = 9$$

Divide by 9:

$$x = 1$$

Therefore

$$1 - 1/\infty = 1$$

$$1/\infty = 0$$

Quiz

2 Which of the following fractions is the **smallest**:

a) $\frac{1}{3}$ b) $\frac{2}{5}$ c) $\frac{4}{9}$

1 a) If you slice a pizza into **8 pieces, eating 3 slices**, what **fraction** of the pizza do you have left?

3 You have a chocolate bar with **12 pieces**. You give **half** of it to a friend then eat **two thirds** of the rest. **How many pieces** do you have left?

4 Convert the following **fractions into decimals:**

a) $\frac{1}{8}$ b) $\frac{4}{5}$ c) $\frac{1}{3}$

b) You slice two pizzas into **quarters, and eat 1 piece** from each. What **fraction of the total amount** of pizza have you eaten.

5 Convert the following **decimals into fractions** in their simplest terms:

a) 0.25   b) 0.7   c) 0.111...

28

6 For their lunch rations, **8 workers** have **6 loaves** of bread to share between them. What is the

minimum number of pieces

of bread you can make to give **equal shares** to all ten workers?

7 In a sale, all clothes are

reduced in price

by $^1/_3$. Moira buys a dress, a pair of boots and a blouse. At full price the dress costs **£60**, the boots cost **£105** and the blouse costs **£45**. How much does Moira pay **in total** in the sale?

8 You are running a market stall selling posters and have the following expenses: You must give $^1/_3$ of your takings **to pay for the stall**. You must give $^2/_5$ of **your takings** to the poster supplier. If you sell **30 posters** at **£5** each,

how much

money do you make?

9 In the US, drill bit sizes are measured in fractions of an inch. The fraction is always expressed in the simplest form. Here are five different sizes:

$$\frac{3}{64}, \frac{1}{4}, \frac{1}{16}, \frac{1}{8}, \frac{3}{32}$$

a) Arrange the drill bits in **order of size**, with the smallest first.

b) Drill bit sizes are sometimes expressed as decimals. If $\frac{1}{64}$ is equal to 0.015625, what are the **decimal conversions** of the five drill bit sizes, from the smallest to largest?

10 A combination lock has three digits, each taking the value of 0–9. How many possible **combinations** are there?

11 The following messages have been scrambled into a code by **replacing one letter** with another found next to it in the alphabet. Can you **crack the codes** and work out what they say? What is the **cypher** in each case?

a) L Z S G R   H R   D U D Q X V G D Q D

b) T F D S F U   D N E F

12 a) Which of the following rules describes the repeated step used to make this **fractal carpet** (below)?

i) Divide each light square into nine equal squares and make the middle square dark.

ii) Divide each light square into 16 equal squares and make the four squares in the middle dark.

iii) Divide each light square into nine squares and make the diagonal squares dark.

b) If step one creates the first dark square, how many steps are shown in the drawing?

Glossary

Complex number
A number that contains a term that is a multiple of $\sqrt{-1}$. Also known as i, $\sqrt{-1}$ is known as the unit imaginary number.

Cryptography
The study of how to make or break secret codes. The process of turning a message into a secret code is called encryption.

Cypher
A mathematical procedure used to produce an encrypted message.

Decimal
Describes the number system that is based on multiples of ten. A decimal fraction has a denominator that is a multiple of ten: for instance, tenths, hundredths or thousandths.

Exponential rate
Growth that becomes faster and faster as the number that is increasing becomes bigger.

Factorisation
The breaking down of a number into smaller numbers that will make that number when multiplied together. Prime factorisation breaks a number down into a series of prime numbers.

Infinitesimal
A fraction that is infinitely small. One way of expressing an infinitesimal value is to call it 'one divided by infinity'.

Infinity
A value that cannot be measured as it goes on for ever. It written with the symbol ∞.

Irrational number
A number that cannot be written in the form a/b, where a and b are whole numbers. $\sqrt{2}$ is an irrational number.

Operation
A procedure to be performed on numbers, such as addition, subtraction, multiplication or division.

Paradox
A statement that sounds reasonable, but that leads to impossible or absurd conclusions. In mathematics, a paradox suggests that at some point you have made a logical mistake.

Reciprocal
The reciprocal of a number is the value that, when multiplied by the number, gives the answer 1. To find the reciprocal of a fraction, you swap the numerator and the denominator.

Series
An infinite sequence of numbers.

Similar
Two objects are similar if they have the same shape, even if they are different sizes. To have the same shape, they must have the same internal angles and the same ratios between the lengths of their sides.

Index

Answers

1. a) $^5/_8$ b) You have eaten $^1/_2$ a pizza. You had two pizzas in total, so the fraction of the total is $^1/_2 \div 2 = ^1/_4$
2. a) is the smallest. The lowest common denominator is 45. So: $^1/_3 = ^{15}/_{45}$, $^2/_5 = ^{18}/_{45}$, $^4/_9 = ^{20}/_{45}$
3. You have two pieces left.
4. a) 0.125 b) 0.8 c) 0.333...
5. a) $^1/_4$ b) $^7/_{10}$ c) $^1/_9$
6. Each worker should receive $^6/_8$ of a loaf = $^3/_4$ Using Egyptian fractions, $^3/_4 = ^1/_2 + ^1/_4$, so each worker gets one half and one quarter. Four loaves are sliced in half, and two are sliced into quarters. That makes 16 pieces in total.
7. Total cost at full price = 60 + 105 + 45 = £210 Sale price = 210 × $^2/_3$ = £140
8. Your total takings are 30 × 5 = £150 The fraction you keep is $1 - ^1/_3 - ^2/_5 = (15 - 5 - 6) / 15 = ^4/_{15}$, $^4/_{15}$ × 150 = £40
9. a) $^5/_{64}$, $^1/_{16}$, $^5/_{32}$, $^1/_8$, $^1/_4$
b) 0.046875, 0.0625, 0.09375, 0.125, 0.25
10. 1,000
11. a) MATHS IS EVERYWHERE. Cypher: move back one along the alphabet.
b) SECRET CODE. Cypher: move forwards one along the alphabet.
12. a) i) b) The drawing shows the fractal after four steps.